Château de Emotion

AF624743

Harshita Pandey

BookLeaf Publishing

Presentation by *BookLeaf Publishing*

Web: www.bookleafpub.com

E-mail: info@bookleafpub.com

ISBN: 9789357215725

First edition 2023

DEDICATION

To,

mosht löd and the Pandeys

ACKNOWLEDGEMENT

Having been someone who has been keen to try out new things from a very young age, I'm immensely grateful that my family has not only always had my back but propelled me to achieve the best in all the avenues I stepped foot in. A firm hand holds astonishing power, sufficient to make the sun set in the east. To have those 3 firms hands and 2 firm paws guide me through all my endeavours serves as a source of strength to me. I'm thankful for my friends who have encouraged me to write that extra article, draft that first page to now get published for the third time. I'm grateful for my mentors, teachers and professors who saw the potential in me and paved the most suitable path for me to take. Thank you to all those who supported me through and through.

Whisk Away

A smile so frail
A look so gaunt
A pile of unfinished lists
And a fear to fail
Curtail her mind, cause a haunt

Maybe dabbling in doubt
A lingering flicker of uncertainty
Bind her, make her own values flout
Confusion makes resolution scanty

But through it all
A whisker and a purr
Will never let her fall
Will never let her deter
Soft-pawed sneaking
Faint meow of reassurance
A warm, well-baked loaf
Would all the worry away, soak

Love's Living Proof

Her unfathomable desires
Her glistening smile
She has much affection to give
For all she loves, she would go the extra mile

She rises with the sun in the dawn
She grinds away with her juggling
One task after another, one more thing
Till she's assembled the flawless, she'd pick on

Her smile would melt the sun
Her touch would carry a tranquil breeze
Her care would heal all scars
Her serenity would make one freeze

I cannot help but dote upon her
A manifestation of elegance, hard work and pragmatism
A mother who is not by anything deterred
A living proof of altruism

A Selfless Man of Intention

He writes away on his desk
He chants his solemn prayers
He treads ahead, firm and resolute
His confidence and faith, whole and absolute

In his car he drives
His job and his responsibilities
In his mind he writes
All his work he carries out in invisibility
His actions he seamlessly steers
His efforts are sequential and planned
At the drop of a hat, at the glint of your fear
Right by you he is ready to stand

He radiates love and values family
He gives away selflessly and happily
A man inclined to adventure
A man serving as a backbone of support
A father so relentless, ready to venture
When he's here, you can fight the whole world
with no effort

Chaos & Toffees

you long to meander into the past
where responsibilities didn’t chase
when at the floor you would blankly gaze
oh but the passage of time, it happened so fast

back when you didn't have to think twice
just to ask for something
back when using a pen for the first time
brought you profound excitement
back when the din of the bell set you free
back when letters were only alphabets
and not equations to you and me

drained from the demand of being older
turning up empty-pocketed at the bus stop
tired of the familiar taste in the food
you yearn to run back into childhood
after everything you drop
when the consequence of our actions was merely a word of caution
and the birth of the worry lines was the least of our distractions
every step is fragile, the flicker of laughter is faint
chaos and toffees would be life's only shade of paint

Plumeria

A skip in my step and glistening eyes
As I inhale the fresh bloom of plumeria
I watch myself linger instead of going inside
Swelling with love for this life in the exurbia
Each passing moment is a glimpse and yet a
drawn out movie
There's nothing more I'd love than to bring it to a
standstill
And see myself grow my roots in the lap of
nature's ingenuity

Scaffold of a Wave

a soft reflection of the screen in the eyes
a stature so tough yet so delicate
a childish excitement echoed in the voice
and mindful to all details so intricate

whilst everyone ran the rat race of time
he cuffed the ticking on his wrist
a logical being of reason
taking calculated and steady risks

what runs amok in his mind
as he upholds himself in stillness and serenity?
perhaps something strategic, to banish
uncertainty
and a thousand ways of being kind he would
find

as loud as a wave
the traits of a mystic
an epitome of patience
he remains resolute
an everlasting scaffold of support
his affection never wavers

Impending Dues

a faint giggle from the back
the flipping of pages and revision sheets
the furious tapping away at the keyboard
piles of unopened conversations in a stack
perhaps a forgotten assignment
maybe some cluelessness in clarity
the chugging of the 3rd coffee cup
deadlines, worry and fatigue keeping you up

yet as you pass by these people
all you see is commonality complementing
diversity
whether you assess 0s and 1s
or study neural circuitry
the differences may be vast but still there
as we sludge on through the wear and tear

Safety Net

oh I wish I could set me free
from the lurking thoughts and anxiety
untether myself from the weight of words
be on my own, not one amongst the herd

just as I venture close
to the threshold of worry
a whisper of hope in prose
would lower the barbed wires of that territory

these people who hold me tight
pull me into a warm ball of a hug
make me laugh, scare away the fright
snap me back to the present with a soft tug
they fill my days with colours of safety
sometimes would make adventurous decisions hasty
but when I turn back around and see
I know that they'll always be there for me

Celestial Mirror

a hesitant gaze into the standing silver
reveals the latent spots and lines
the ones that you have longed to hide
to keep the curtains closed, you tried
why does fear lurk within?
have you been subjected to nothing but scrutiny?
did it always stir between your thoughts a mutiny?
to silence the malicious monologue, you must begin

you are what you need to be, someone benign
don't uphold the labels and let them you, define
just as you admire the moon and its divinity
to do to yourself, you must go beyond infinity
your presence calming and your existence celestial
no person can ever the grace of the moon dull

Effortlessness

Never realised what effortless meant
Until away from you I went
The quick exchanged glances
The confused and uncanny dances
A voice so loud and distant
An echo and pitch mismatched
The anarchy we reigned at home
I would've cherished, had I known
What effortless was

Our experiments with taste buds
Be it the kimchi or the kombucha
The horror movie marathons
The car rides where we'd sing along
In these moments I would've settled
Had I any idea about the effortless

It was always with you
Even trouble, together we'd get into
The understanding between us, continental
So perfectly coordinated, never accidental

To go with the flow so easily
You make it effortless, so readily

The Gravity of Words

if we really mull it over
give it some time and see
how did we start clinging onto the weight of words?
when did we let that dictate our happiness?
why put on a label when it only gives you hurt?
where do you take yourself in helplessness?
why do you dwell on validation in "good"?
since when did it tell you what you can feel or
should?

don't tangle yourself in this thread
there may be far too many strings attached
carefully you should tread
thank the sentiment and from the rest, stay detached
you have no moulds to fit into
you don't need to be defined
you aren't limited to a word or two
already freely flowing and refined

Highway Lights

The brown noise emanates
As the engine of the car whirrs
The highway light your face illuminates
Maybe jars you awake or causes a stir

The backseat of the car
Reserved a spot for you
The late night retreats from afar
Back to the comfort of home, true

The highway lights prance around
Their light rays spotlighting your face through
the window
The moon racing your car as you watch in a
puzzled frown
The empty streets really letting the control go

Cinnamon Twists

the whiff of cinnamon settled on my hoodie
the dancing fairy lights suspended from the ceiling
feet socked up in red wool for insulation
pine cones and trees set up for the season
the impending fear of missing ornaments
a venturing threat of paws may be the detriment

the late night squiggling on letters
wishing for everyone something better
a curled up cat asking for me to pet her
fur lined the sleeves of my sweater
the golden shimmer from the wrapper
the chime of bells and carols the spirit pamper
mysterious packages and boxes under the tree
for I knew it was my Santa who shared my glee

Orbit of Proximity

every move, calculated
every thought, strategic
every possibility in my plan I inculcated
every missed chance, almost tragic

I honed my forte of research
deployed all the skills I needed
to end up in your orbit, for a chance I'd search
no matter the challenge, I would never have retreated

perfectly aligned latitudes of this plane
uncanny resemblance of the timing
never let anything intercept this thought train
till I'd clutch you, I'd keep on climbing

To Learn

stepping outside the threshold with bated breath
filled up with anxiety and a little bit of dread
all those articles and all the books I'd read
would they in preparation help me tread?

no advice or piece of writing
could teach me how to adult
could fuel my confidence in tumult
could help me navigate through what's trifling

the greatest teacher is experience
to push me through dark times with incandescence
to teach me how to solo travel
to get to difficult conversations unravel
to keep a check on my budgets and finances
to learn the difference between right and wrong
glances
to place in deserving people my trust
to get what's rightfully mine with vigour and thrust

Me, all along

If it wasn't for me
who would watch my back?
who would stand guard like a scarecrow?
in my field of feelings where winds of trust would blow?
ready to prance and push away those willing to attack

if it wasn't for me
who would tell me to take that risk?
to point out the sub-clause under the asterisk?
who would tell me what's mine to gain?
to read between the lines and save the pain?

if it wasn't for me
who would get me through rough winds at the sea?
who would look over from the mast and find a path that's free?
who would guide my ship through the high tide?
and as I dock at the shore of safety, take a proud stride?

if it wasn't for me
who would treat me like a child?
tell me that a mistake is only mild?
to pat my own back and encourage
call out what's wrong with outrage?

it took me time to pause and notice
I'd evolved from a mere novice
I had learnt how to safeguard my fields
I had understood how to decipher words
I had mastered my ship's sails
I had nurtured my innocence

Red Room

with a sigh i tuck away
this photographic moment in my memory album
the glint of the red on your underdeveloped films
hidden within the dark crevices are your shameful secrets
a misconstrued emotion, a frame of regrets

not all your shades rose to the surface
lurking in the shadows were your photo negatives
little did i know, little did i see
before it came to light, i should've chosen to flee
with an obscure lens you crept close
captured my vulnerability, you stood so tall
hindsight reveals a latent desire
your photos might as well have been a poorly written satire
i mounted to the wall your portrait of disguise
oh how I wish I knew those decisions i would despise

a reel of lies i watched you spin
whilst giving me those paper cuts i never saw you flinch
watch me flood your red room with a light so bright
you'll come to believe with me you should've never picked a strife

Beauty Forged in Existence

a tinge of blue painted the sky
the wind as cold as shards of ice
leaves bejewelled with dew
calm over me it drew

I watched as the sun ventured over the peak
the warmth radiating like a soft glow
the sun climbing the sky, timid and meek
the trees blanketed in the light as they stood in rows

a benign breeze touched my face
a coat of wind I stood within
enveloped in the warmth it carried from the sun
the fresh green smell I could feel sink in

I basked in the silence
a faint bird song echoed from the distance
I stood in the quiet, I stood in awe
admiring nature's trinkets
beauty from each element you could draw
any threat to this elegance I shall be ready to picket